# POSITION
## *Pieces*

for violin and piano
Intermediate repertoire in 2nd, 3rd and 4th positions

*Neue Lagen für Violine und Klavier*
Spielstücke mittlerer Schwierigkeit in der zweiten, dritten und vierten Lage

All pieces edited and arranged by/Alle Stücke herausgegeben und bearbeitet von

**Marguerite Wilkinson and Alan Gout**

Standin' in the need of Prayer   *Spiritual*   2
Sweet Genevieve   *Tucker*   3
A Wonderful Guy   *Rodgers & Hammerstein*   4
Kalamatianos   *Bass*   6
Piece   *Elgar*   8
Bali Ha'i   *Rodgers & Hammerstein*   10
Two Minuets   *Montéclair*   12
Danse des Baronnes   *Tchaikovsky*   14
Minuetto   *Flackton*   16
Plaisir d'Amour   *Martini*   18
Wedding Dance   *Grieg*   22
Berceuse   *Blake*   24
Hornpipe in Sand Dance Style   *Anon.*   25
I know de Lord's laid His hands on me   *Spiritual*   26
Country Dance   *Beethoven*   28
March   *Anon.*   29
Song of Twilight   *Nakada*   30

**FABER *ff* MUSIC**

All pieces © 1995 by Faber Music Ltd unless otherwise stated
This edition first published in 1995 by Faber Music Ltd
3 Queen Square London WC1N 3AU
Cover design by Lynette Williamson
Music processed by Wessex Music Services
German translations by Dorothee Göbel
Printed in England by Halstan and Co Ltd

ISBN 0 571 51505 3

In order to achieve secure intonation, the student must understand the relative placings of the fingers across the strings when playing in different keys and positions. By 'staying put' in one position for a substantial stretch of music, the geography of that position is quickly learned, enabling the student to tackle the adventure of moving up and down the fingerboard with confidence.

These pieces have been chosen not only for this purpose, but also to present a wide variety of interesting and unusual repertoire from the baroque period to our own time. We hope that skill and enjoyment will thereby go hand in hand.

Marguerite Wilkinson
Alan Gout

Zur Erlangung einer sicheren Intonation braucht der Schüler Verständnis für die jeweilige Positionierung der Finger auf den Saiten bei unterschiedlichen Tonarten und Lagen. Dadurch, daß der Schüler sich in einem Musikstück über einen längeren Abschnitt hin in einer Lage bewegt, erlernt er den genauen Ort, die "Geographie" dieser Lage schnell. Mit diesen Kenntnissen ausgestattet kann er sich dann auch vertrauensvoll auf das Abenteuer einlassen, die Hand auf dem Griffbrett nach oben und unten zu bewegen.

Die vorliegenden Stücke wurden aber nicht nur aus diesem Grund, sondern auch ausgesucht, um eine große Breite interessanter und ungewöhnlicher Stücke vom Barock bis in unsere Zeit vorzustellen. Wir hoffen, daß das Erlernen technischer Fähigkeiten und der Spaß bei der Sache Hand in Hand gehen.

Marguerite Wilkinson
Alan Gout

2

½ , 1st & 3rd Positions

# Standin' in the need of Prayer

Spiritual

# Sweet Genevieve

Henry Tucker
(c. 1826 - 1882)

# A Wonderful Guy

Richard Rodgers &
Oscar Hammerstein

# Kalamatianos

Philip Bass

# Piece

Edward Elgar
(1857 - 1934)

3rd Position

# Bali Ha'i

Richard Rodgers &
Oscar Hammerstein

3rd Position

# Two Minuets

Michel Pignolet
de Montéclair
(1667 - 1737)

**Minuet II**

D.C. Minuet I al Fine

# Danse des Baronnes

3rd Position

P. I. Tchaikovsky
(1840 - 1893)

Tempo di Gavotte ( ♩ = 126)

# POSITION PIECES · BOOK 2

## VIOLIN PART

# POSITION PIECES · BOOK 2

**VIOLIN PART**

½, 1st & 3rd Positions

## Standin' in the need of Prayer

Spiritual

½ & 1st Position

## Sweet Genevieve

Henry Tucker
(c. 1826 - 1882)

This music is copyright. Photocopying is illegal.

3rd Position

# A Wonderful Guy

Richard Rodgers &
Oscar Hammerstein

3rd Position

# Kalamatianos

Philip Bass

3rd Position

# Piece

Edward Elgar
(1857 - 1934)

# Bali Ha'i

3rd Position

Richard Rodgers &
Oscar Hammerstein

Moderato ( ♩ = 100 )

3rd Position

# Two Minuets

Michel Pignolet
de Montéclair
(1667 - 1737)

3rd Position

# Danse des Baronnes

P. I. Tchaikovsky
(1840 - 1893)

2nd Position

# Minuetto

William Flackton
(1709 - 1798)

2nd Position

# Plaisir d'Amour

Giovanni Battista Martini
(1706 - 1784)

2nd Position

# Wedding Dance

Edvard Grieg
(1843 - 1907)

3rd Position

# Berceuse

Howard Blake

2nd Position

# Hornpipe in Sand Dance Style

Vigoroso (♩ = 138)

Anon.

2nd Position

# I know de Lord's laid His hands on me

Spiritual

Lively (♩ = 138)

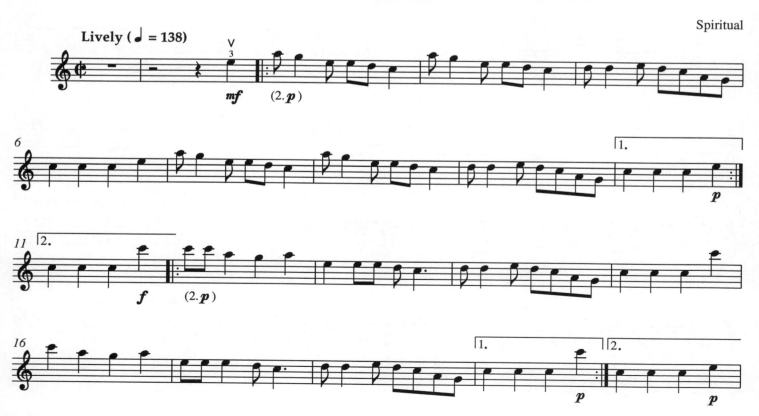

(2. *f*)

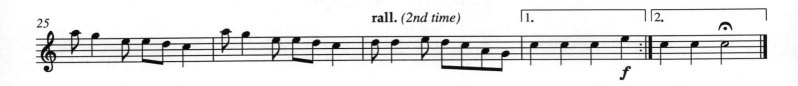

rall. *(2nd time)*

4th Position

# Country Dance

L. van Beethoven
(1770 - 1827)

Moderato ( ♩ = 100)

4th Position

# March

Anon., c. 1790

Marcato ( ♩ = 96)

12

4th Position

# Song of Twilight

**Tranquillo ( ♩ = 60)**

Yoshinao Nakada
(b. 1923)

# Minuetto

William Flackton
(1709 - 1798)

2nd Position

2nd Position

# Plaisir d'Amour

Giovanni Battista Martini
(1706 - 1784)

# Wedding Dance

Edvard Grieg
(1843 - 1907)

**Moderato ( ♩ = 84)**

23

3rd Position

# Berceuse

Howard Blake

Andantino ( ♩. = 69 )

2nd Position

# Hornpipe in Sand Dance Style

Anon.

2nd Position

# I know de Lord's laid His hands on me

Spiritual

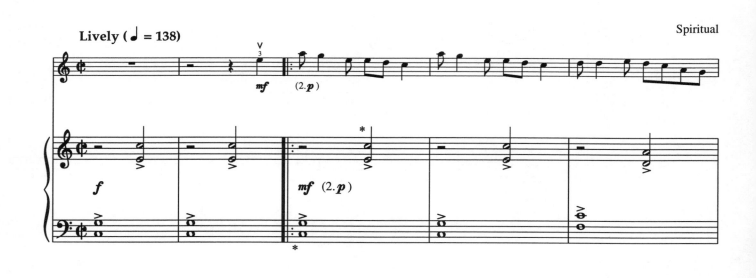

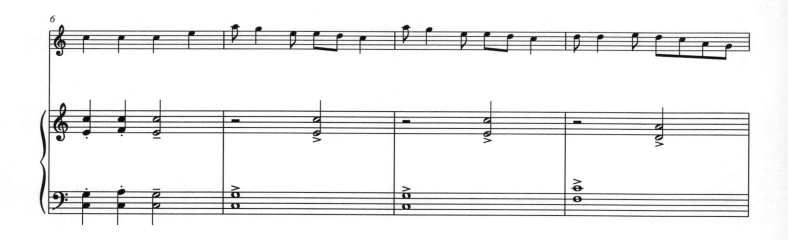

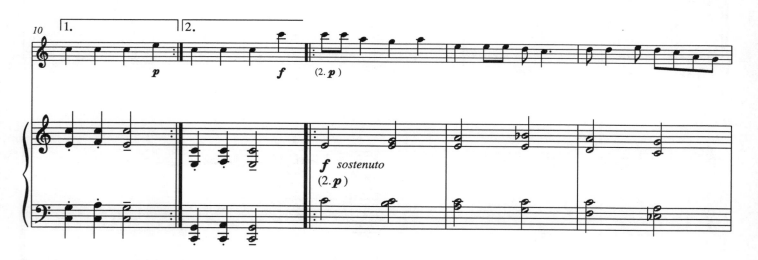

\* Play both hands down an octave for the repeat (bars 3-9 inclusive)

# Country Dance

4th Position

L. van Beethoven
(1770 - 1827)

# March

4th Position

Anon., c. 1790

4th Position

# Song of Twilight

Yoshinao Nakada
(b. 1923)